OCEAN TOURS

D1362384

WRITTEN AND ILLUSTRATED BY
BROOKE BESSESEN

look who lives in the ocean!

Splashing and Dashing, Nibbling and Quibbling, Blending and Fending

ARIZONA
HIGHWAYS

MIKE WALLACE

As a naturalist, Brooke Bessesen studies the world's biomes and diverse species that inhabit them. Most enchanting for her is the oceanic realm, where she has been eye-to-eye with whales, dolphins, sea turtles, sharks, and other wondrous animals.

Brooke worked at the Phoenix Zoo as a certified veterinary technician and on-camera naturalist. For more than two decades she has also served as a wildlife rescue volunteer.

For many years she produced television programming, including the top-rated weekly series **A Brighter Day,** and stories for National Geographic Channel, Style Network, and Discovery Health.

Her unique and colorful illustrations begin as pencil drawings, which are scanned into a computer and colorized with digitally manipulated fabrics.

Brooke is the award-winning author of two other children's books, **Look Who Lives in the Desert!** and **Zachary Z. Packrat and His Amazing Collections,** both published by **Arizona Highways**.

She strives to educate and empower young and not-so-young readers alike. To see photos and video of animals, learn more about Brooke's writing and illustrations, download free book-based curriculum, or find out how you can help wildlife, explore www.brookebessesen.com.

In memory of Warren Iliff (1936-2006), a charismatic visionary, devoted animal advocate, and kind-hearted friend, whose acute editorial eye and sincere support assisted this manuscript to publication.

ACKNOWLEDGMENTS

My heartfelt thanks to everyone who has cradled and cared for this book:
to the team at **Arizona Highways** for your dedication to excellence;
to Mary — your talent and passion have given my books wings;
to the conservation scientists who allowed me time in the field for
expanding my knowledge and experience;
to Annie, for helping me edit and organize the facts;
to Anthony and Mindi, for the tools to create my illustrations;
to my writers' group, for your dynamism and trusted insight;
to my little friend Donnie, for your remarkable artistic sensibility;
to Ryn, for the sheer enthusiasm that kept me afloat during the storms;
to family and friends, who have offered unwavering encouragement;
and to Kevin, my sweet mouse, for always believing in me!

Designer: Mary Winkelman Velgos
Book Editor: Bob Albano

Printed in Singapore

FOR YOUNG IMAGINATIONS and ARIZONA HIGHWAYS are trademarks of the Arizona Department of Transportation, parent of **Arizona Highways**.

Published by the Book Division of **Arizona Highways**® magazine, a monthly publication of the Arizona Department of Transportation, 2039 West Lewis Avenue, Phoenix, Arizona 85009.
Telephone: (602) 712-2200
Web site: www.arizonahighways.com

Publisher: Win Holden
Editor: Robert Stieve
Senior Editor / Books: Randy Summerlin

Most people love the ocean! We are captivated by its stunning beauty, depth, and mystique. More than half the world's human population lives near the coast, and those who don't often travel to vacation along its beaches.

Twice a day, on every continent, the ocean tides rise and fall along the shoreline. And strong currents, like water highways, push warm and cold water around the globe. Such fluctuations in movement and temperature help determine our weather.

Exactly why is the ocean blue? Partly, because it reflects the sky. But mostly, the color blue is least absorbed by water, and tiny particles suspended in the water refract (bounce) that color back to the surface. As the water deepens and less light is able to penetrate, the color turns from blue to black.

The ocean is home to millions of animals, including the mammals, birds, reptiles, fishes, and invertebrates featured in this book. Some scientists estimate that 80 percent of all life is found beneath the ocean surface. The largest living structure on Earth, the Great Barrier Reef off the coast of Australia, can even be seen from space!

Not only is the ocean gorgeous to look at — and fun to play in — but it's also the most important body of water on the planet. The ocean provides food, energy, oxygen, and minerals for all living things, so there is good reason to keep it clean and healthy. Yet it's being gravely damaged. Global warming and pollution are altering water quality and quickly destroying marine habitats. Animal species are disappearing.

If we truly love the ocean, we must work together to protect it. I hope you will enjoy reading **Look Who Lives in the Ocean!**, and then help me educate others about the ocean and its magnificent creatures. Since I contribute some of the monies you pay for this book to support wildlife conservation, we are already joining hands to make a difference.

— Brooke Bessesen

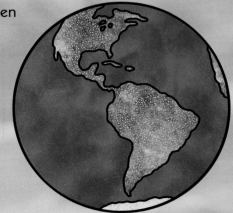

The ocean provides
a magnificent view —
miles and miles
of fabulous blue.

But under the surface
exists so much more,
a wonderful world
we can't see from the shore,
with history and mystery ...
and fishes galore.

The ocean covers roughly 70 percent of the Earth's surface and holds about 97 percent of the planet's water supply.

The ocean actually consists of five connected oceans:

the Pacific, the largest and deepest, covering one-third of the planet;

the Atlantic, the second-largest and shaped like an S;

the Indian, third-largest and the warmest, shaped like an upside down V;

the Southern, sometimes called the Antarctic because it surrounds the continent of Antarctica;

the Arctic, the smallest and made up of mostly ice.

Seas are smaller branches of the ocean that are partly enclosed by land.

The Red Sea has a seasonal red hue because of a type of algae that blooms in it, and the Black Sea is blackish because of high levels of a substance called hydrogen sulfide.

The Mariana Trench is the ocean's deepest point — the bottom is almost 7 miles below the surface. The pressure there is 8 tons per square inch, about equal to one human holding 50 jumbo jets.

FASCINATING FACTS

BROOKE BESSESEN

There are more than 30,000 species of fish — most live in the ocean. That's more than all the mammals, birds, reptiles, and amphibians put together.

Some fish live in tightly coordinated groups called shoals (also called schools). Tens of thousands of fish can live in one shoal. Shoals confuse predators that try to follow just one fish.

Shoals can move in unison because each fish has "lateral lines" of neuromasts (sensory cells), which run the length of a fish's body on both sides. These cells detect minute changes in water pressure and movement, so individuals can feel and respond to the group almost instantly.

Most fish have a bony skeleton supported on a spine. Their skin is covered with tiny, transparent scales that overlap for flexibility. Fins provide movement and steering, and a swim bladder (inflatable sac of gases) keeps them neutrally buoyant (not sinking or floating).

To breathe, fish absorb oxygen from water by sucking water over gills, which are tightly folded surfaces rich in blood vessels to carry oxygen into the bloodstream. The area inside the gills is 10 times larger than that of the fish's skin.

Many fish communicate by making sounds, but usually humans can't hear them.

FASCINATING FACTS

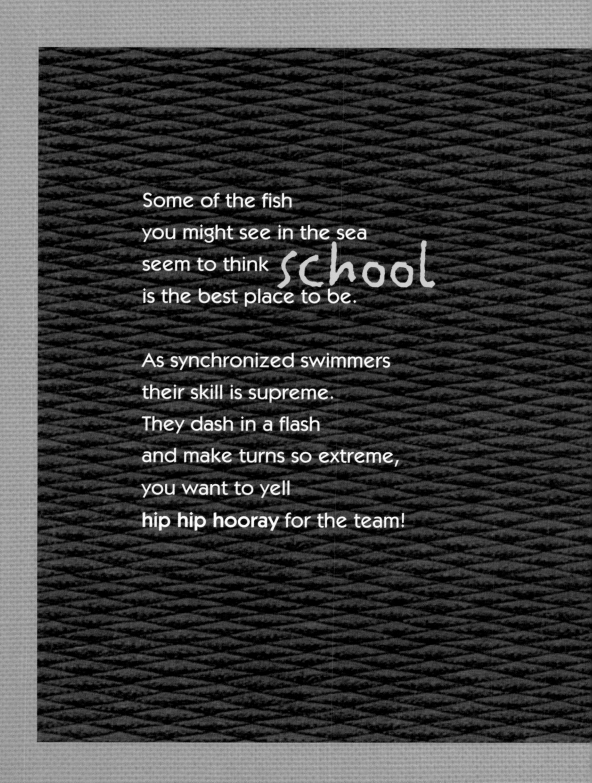

Some of the fish
you might see in the sea
seem to think *school*
is the best place to be.

As synchronized swimmers
their skill is supreme.
They dash in a flash
and make turns so extreme,
you want to yell
hip hip hooray for the team!

A lobster

works night shift
from dusk until dawn,
cleaning each section
before she moves on.

She dines on the finds,
and her diet's complete,
but imagine enjoying
the goodies she'd eat —
like decaying meat.
Mmmm … **bon appétit!**

CAUTION
WET FLOOR

Lobsters are invertebrate scavengers (they eat dead things), but they also catch and eat fresh food including fish, urchins, clams, mussels, crabs, and sometimes other lobsters. They are usually nocturnal (active at night) and hide by day in rocky crevices with only their antennae sticking out.

A lobster has around 40 appendages. There are usually 10 on its head, including manipulatory (hand-like) mouthparts; 16 on the thorax (body), including walking legs; and on the tail, 10 short legs called swimmerets and two flattened legs that make up the tail fan.

Lobsters range in color from reddish to green, orange, yellow, or blue. As crustaceans,

continental plates

CRUSTY'S
CLEANING SERVICE!
"clean to Me, Me to clean"
INVOICE
Plan: continuous
Fee: "food"
"payment will be
collected during
the worker's shift

SPRAY
AWAY

lobsters are arthropods (from Greek words for "jointed foot"). Lobsters must molt (discard their old exoskeleton) in order to grow.

Using muscles in its abdomen and tail, a lobster can quickly propel backwards to escape danger.

When some lobster species are frightened, they make a grating or buzzing sound by rubbing the hard pads at the base of their antennae against special ridges on their head. This behavior is called stridulation.

Lobster eggs are attached to the female's body on the outside of her shell, and a mother can carry as many as 63,000 eggs for up to two years before they hatch.

FASCINATING FACTS

HERB SEGARS

Humpback whales are mammals found in every ocean on Earth. A thick layer of blubber (fat cells) protects them from extreme temperature changes as they migrate between cool, feeding waters in summer and warmer, breeding waters in winter.

Humpbacks breathe air through paired blowholes (two nostrils that are close together) on top of the head. They can grow up to 53 feet long and weigh 25 to 40 tons. Instead of teeth, these whales have 270 to 400 baleen (a horny tissue) plates to strain water from the schools of fish and krill (tiny, shelled creatures) they eat. A humpback whale can hold 500 to 1,000 gallons in its mouth.

"Whale songs" can be heard more than 20 miles away and last up to 20 minutes. Singing is one way whales communicate with each other. The male is the main singer, and the songs include distinct themes and melodies. The song patterns change, making new songs every few years. Yet there is still much about whale songs that we don't understand.

The markings on the underside of a humpback's tail fluke are as unique as a human fingerprint and can be used by researchers to identify individuals.

FASCINATING FACTS

You'll never hear
a more beautiful song
than one from a **humpback**
that's fifty feet long.

He belts the best ballad.
He croons the best tune.
He plays a lagoon
by the light of the moon.
But when he performs,
do the girl **whales** swoon?

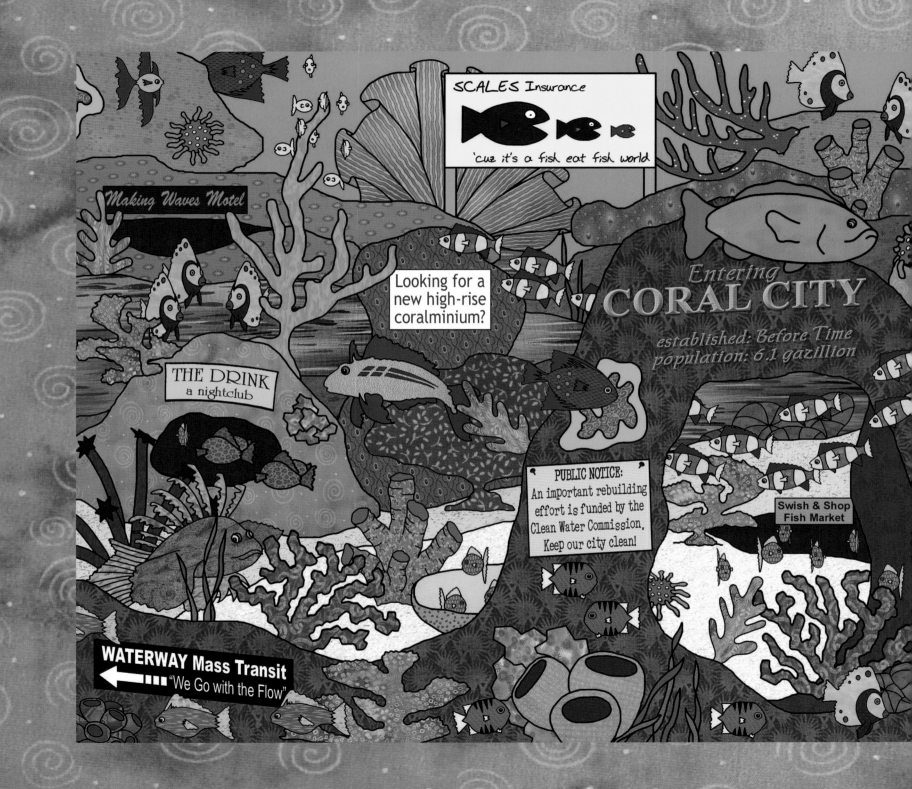

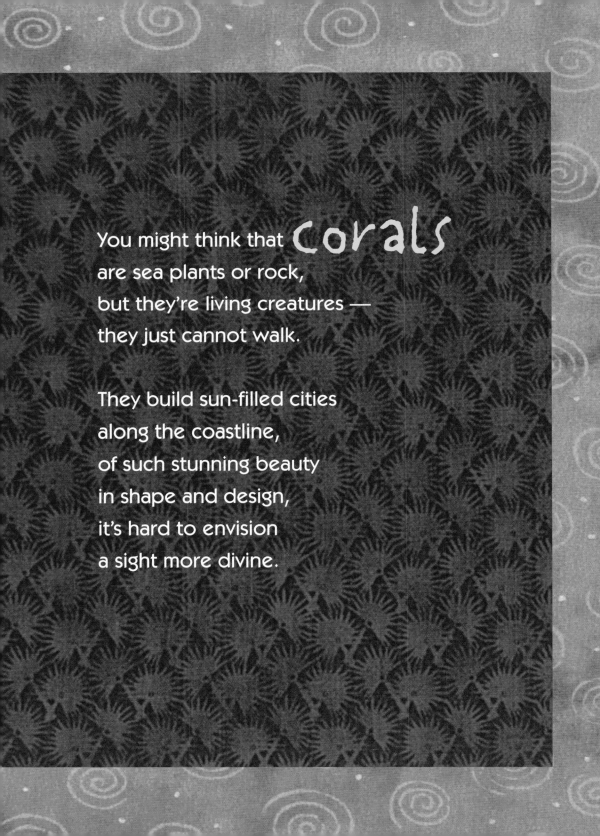

You might think that *Corals*
are sea plants or rock,
but they're living creatures —
they just cannot walk.

They build sun-filled cities
along the coastline,
of such stunning beauty
in shape and design,
it's hard to envision
a sight more divine.

Corals are animals — not plants or rocks. These invertebrates grow in beautiful shapes, colors, and sizes, and form huge, living, multi-generational landscape structures called reefs that provide food and shelter for thousands of other aquatic animals.

Corals grow in the topmost layer of ocean water called the euphotic (or sunlit) zone. They are killed by environmental changes and by humans stepping on them.

Corals eat zooplankton (miniscule animals that drift on currents) that they capture with tiny tentacles. Their food is moved to the mouth using mucus (sticky fluid) and cilia (tiny hairs). Most corals are nocturnal (active at night) and keep their tentacles retracted during the day.

Corals also have a symbiotic relationship with single-celled algae called zooxanthellae. That means they help each other survive. The algae live in the cells of the coral and produce food for the coral through photosynthesis (turning sunlight to energy). In return, the coral provides protection and access to light for the algae.

At certain times, corals release their spores (reproductive cells) into the water for a mass spawning. The zygote (fertilized egg) develops into a larva (baby) and settles onto the bottom to begin a new colony.

FASCINATING FACTS

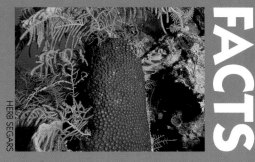

HERB SEGARS

All 7 species of sea turtle are endangered. The largest sea turtle is the leatherback, which can be more than 8 feet long and weigh more than a ton. Leatherbacks eat jellyfish, and some are killed because they mistake floating plastic bags (human litter) for food.

Sea turtles are air-breathing reptiles and must swim to the surface regularly to breathe, but they can stay submerged for up to an hour. Very few predators can bite through the shell of an adult sea turtle, but sea turtles cannot draw their arms and legs into their shells like land turtles can.

A pregnant female returns to the exact beach where she was hatched. She digs a pit in the sandy beach and lays 70 to 170 eggs, covering them before returning to the sea. Weeks later, the baby sea turtles break out of the nest, scuttle down the beach, and into the water. Most sea turtles do not reach adulthood. Sea turtles are mostly solitary (live alone) and can live more than 80 years.

Some sea turtles are omnivorous (meat and plant eaters). Others, when they are young, eat small sea creatures but become vegetarians (plant eaters) as they mature.

FASCINATING FACTS

BROOKE BESSESEN

A giant *sea turtle*
sports great plates of shell,
and her long, lanky flippers
propel her quite well.

She goes up and takes in
a big breath of air,
then slowly descends
on her way to somewhere …
Hats off to this
sea diver extraordinaire.

FASCINATING FACTS

BROOKE BESSESEN

Seagull is the common name given to gull species that live by the ocean.

The birds are omnivores (meat and plant eaters) that dine primarily on fish, insects, and water organisms. Using wind currents seagulls can fly very low over the ocean, snatching small fish from the water. Their webbed feet help them paddle when they float on the ocean surface.

Seagulls are also opportunistic scavengers and will eat carrion (dead animals) and other decaying matter, including garbage. While they are sometimes considered pests, they are quite helpful in keeping beaches clean.

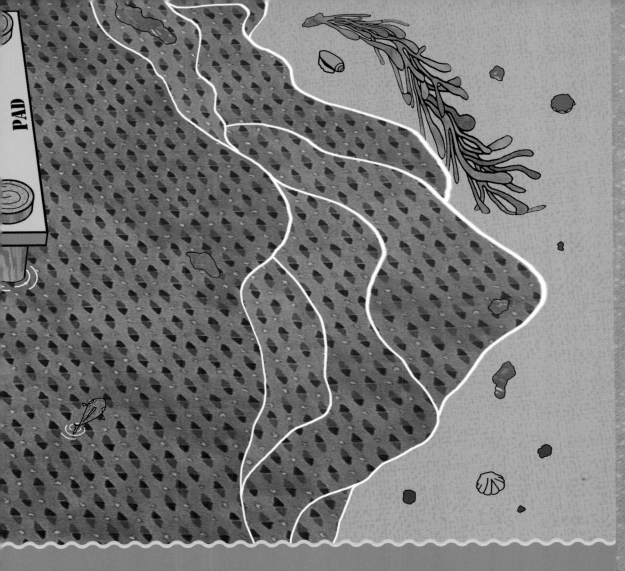

This **gull's**
on the lookout.
He's ready to act.
In fact his fine timing
is very exact.

He's like Search & Rescue,
except all **he** saves
are tidbits to eat
from the beaches and waves.
Leftover morsels
and fish are his faves.

A gull defends itself by making loud, harsh calls. It also spreads its wings on the ground to appear bigger to potential predators.

Gulls make nests and lay two to three eggs at a time. The young hatch in about 20 days. Adult gulls can be very protective, even aggressive, when they are taking care of eggs or babies.

The California gull is migratory (travels to different areas) and is Utah's state bird because during a severe cricket infestation in 1848, the "seagulls" saved the state's crops by gorging on the invading insects.

Late in the evening
as darkness sets in,
it's time for the night-light
parade to begin.

Sea jelly floats
are the best in the show.
Drifting on currents,
they shimmer and glow
with long, stinging tentacles
trailing below.

Sea jellies, sometimes called jellyfish, are planktonic (drift on currents). Some can propel themselves by contracting their bell (body), but they still rely on currents. These invertebrates can travel hundreds of miles and are found in all the oceans of the world.

A jelly's tentacles have nematocysts (stinging cells) used to paralyze prey.

The Portuguese man-of-war, which has tentacles that can reach 120 feet long, may look like a jellyfish, but technically it is not.

Some jellies live in the middle layer of ocean waters called the disphotic (or twilight) zone, where there is very little light. These jellies have bioluminescence (their own light or glow), which they produce through a biochemical reaction in their bodies. Only parts of the animal actually light up and usually only when the jelly is disturbed.

A jelly's composition contains more than 95 percent water and has no skeleton, gills, heart, blood, or brain. It does, however, have cells that provide senses of taste and smell.

Jellies hatch from eggs and have short life spans. They are food for many other animals.

FASCINATING FACTS

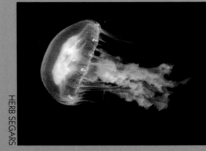

Sharks are fish. They have prominent dorsal (back) fins that sometimes appear above the water. There are at least 350 species of sharks, including the great white shark, which can grow to more than 21 feet long and weigh nearly 3,000 pounds.

A shark will grow new teeth continually throughout its life and may have 3,000 at one time. Teeth in outer rows are the largest and most used, but when these become damaged or lost, teeth from the inner rows move outward.

Some sharks allow reef-dwelling wrasses called "cleaner fish" to remove loose skin, parasites, and food remains from their bodies and even inside their mouths.

Sharks have good eyesight, hearing, and smell (some species can smell a drop of blood in 1 million drops of seawater). They also have electro-perception. Using special sensors on their heads called ampullae (small jelly-filled pores), sharks pick up electromagnetic currents that help them detect prey.

A shark's skeleton is made of cartilage instead of bone. It breathes through gills, and many must keep moving in order to breathe.

FASCINATING FACTS

HERB SEGARS

With thousands of teeth
that are lined up in aisles,
her choppers are whoppers,
so Shark always smiles.

Just think of her dentist,
his horror, his fright,
to try to keep all of those
pearly whites bright.
I'll bet he's quite careful
to do things **just right**.

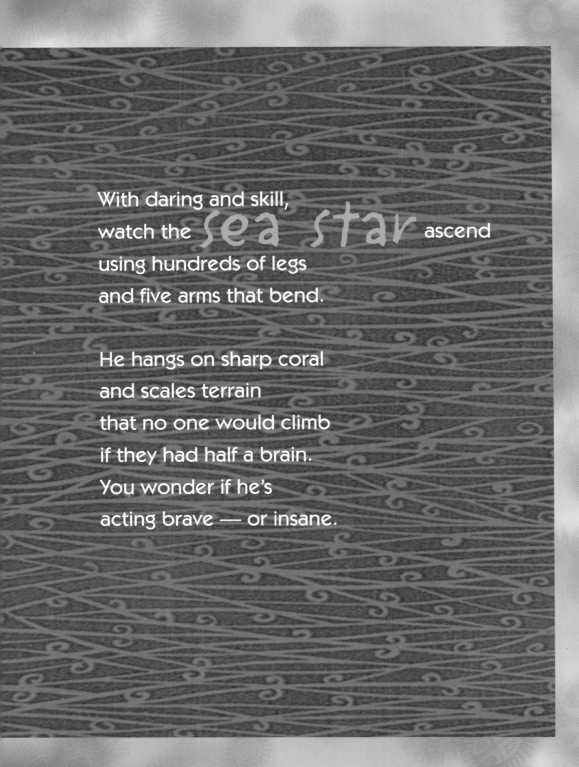

With daring and skill,
watch the *sea star* ascend
using hundreds of legs
and five arms that bend.

He hangs on sharp coral
and scales terrain
that no one would climb
if they had half a brain.
You wonder if he's
acting brave — or insane.

Although sea stars sometimes are called starfish, they are not fish, but invertebrates. They are covered with small spines and are called echinoderms (a word derived from Greek meaning "spiny skin").

The sea star has hundreds of tiny tube feet on its underside that are used for walking, grasping prey, and moving food to its mouth.

A sea star's rays (hollow arms) link to a center disc and often have large, defensive plates. Each ray also has a light-sensitive organ called an eye spot that can detect light and its general direction. If a ray is broken off, it can grow back.

Sea stars move so slowly along the sea-bed that they often look like they're sitting still. They are so strong that they can cling to surfaces while they are inverted (upside down). Typically, sea stars live 3 to 5 years.

Sea stars are voracious predators of clams, oysters, and mussels. The sea stars pry open the shells with slow steady pressure from their legs, spill digestive juices onto their meals, and suck up the material dissolved by the juices.

The five-armed sea star has amazing symmetry: Picture a line dividing one through the middle; no matter which way you turn it, the two halves always will have a perfect balance.

FASCINATING FACTS

At the gateway
where a river meets bay,
a **manatee's**
birthday
comes early in May.

Could she be the mermaid
from which legend grew?
Enchanting young men
on the ships passing through,
and carried away
in the dreams of each crew?

Manatees are gentle mammals. They are thought to be the source of legends about mermaids. Sailors may have seen these quiet creatures beneath the water's surface and imagined them to be mythical fish-people.

Manatees now are extremely endangered. Small isolated populations live where certain warm rivers meet and mix with ocean water in parts of Florida, the Caribbean, Central America, and West Africa. Many of the creatures are killed by collisions with powerboats.

Although they frequently rise to the surface to breathe through their nostrils, manatees can stay submerged for as long as 20 minutes. They make squealing

FRESH WATER

SALT WATER

HAPPY BIRTHDAY!

sounds underwater to communicate with each other.

The manatee, a slow-moving herbivore (plant eater), can grow to 12 feet long and weigh up to 3,500 pounds. As they chew

aquatic vegetation, their molars wear down and new molars form at the back of the mouth, moving forward over time. These are referred to as "marching molars." The manatee's closest land relative is the elephant.

Births occur throughout the year, but the peak season is spring. An infant nurses from milk glands in the mother's armpits. A manatee may live for more than 60 years.

FASCINATING FACTS

HERB SEGARS

Swordfish live in the Atlantic, Pacific, and Indian oceans. They migrate between colder waters in the summer and warmer waters in the winter.

Swordfish can grow up to 15 feet long and weigh nearly 1,200 pounds. One of the fastest fish in the sea, they can travel at speeds of up to 60 mph and even faster in short bursts.

An adult swordfish has no teeth, but its long, sharp upper snout (over one-third of its total body length) is so powerful, it can pierce 2 inches of solid wood.

A swordfish eats mainly squid and small fish like mackerel, herring, and tuna. It dines mostly at night, feeding in deep water by swinging its bill into a school of fish and eating those that are killed, stunned, or wounded.

Swordfish don't have any pelvic fins. Adults also lack scales, making their skin appear shiny. Swordfish are brownish-gray or even blue-purple, with lighter coloring on the underside.

Female swordfish produce tens of millions of eggs. Swordfish can live more than 25 years, but most never reach that age due to commercial fishing.

FASCINATING FACTS

Ahoy! It's the *swordfish*
with his mighty snout.
It's like a long blade
that he slashes about.

At staggering speeds
when he's skimming outright,
his sleek, shiny skin
looks like tin in the light.
With thick muscles flexing,
he's really a sight.

Over the floor Doris
glides with such grace,
on beauty alone
she'd be voted first place.

She wears brilliant colors
that boost her appeal,
and yet no one dares
take her out for a meal,
Cuz one little bite could
become an ordeal.

Dorids (plural for doris) are a type of nudibranch (sea slug) and are related to flatworms and sea hares. They have long, flattened bodies ranging in size from very small to 6 inches long and more than an inch wide.

Most dorids eat sponges and are immune to their powerful toxins. Dorids even incorporate the poisonous chemicals from their prey into their own bodies and use them for defense against predators.

Many dorids are brilliantly colored and bizarrely shaped. Some are bright and showy to warn predators that they taste bad or are poisonous. Others use color for camouflage to help them blend in with their surroundings.

A doris has two sets of structures protruding from its back. Toward the front are rhinophores (sensory antennae) that they use to "smell" chemicals emitted from each other or from their prey. The delicate, feather-looking structures closer to the back end are gills.

Dorids are invertebrates, and like all sea slugs are hermaphrodites (having both male and female organs).

FASCINATING FACTS

HERB SEGARS

A seahorse is actually a fish. Its body is encased in bony rings with armored plates. The seahorse changes colors like a chameleon and has protrusions that provide camouflage in the corals and grasses where it lives.

Seahorses are poor swimmers. The dorsal (back) fin propels them forward, while pectoral fins on the sides of the head control turning and steering. The prehensile (grabbing) tail holds them in place. Many die in storms because they lose their strong holds and reach exhaustion or are washed up on shore.

In seahorses, it is the male that gets pregnant. A female seahorse produces eggs and deposits them into the male's brooding pouch. He carries the young (about 150 to 200 babies at a time) in his pouch for two to six weeks before he gives birth, usually during a full moon.

Seahorse eyes move independently from one another. Seahorses have no teeth and swallow food whole, mostly tiny crustaceans like shrimp that pass by on currents of water.

There are 35 known species of seahorse. They can be found in most temperate and tropical coastal waters and vary in size from 1/4 inch to over a foot tall.

FASCINATING FACTS

HERB SEGARS

Among the long grasses
that sway in the tide,
a *seahorse* has babies
he carried inside.

Yes, you read correctly,
believe it or not,
with this fish the father
delivers each tot.
And there can be hundreds —
poor Dad, that's a lot.

Her flat body waves
like a flag in the breeze
as she slips through the
shadowy water with ease.

If **Stingray** decides
that she shouldn't be seen,
she slides down and hides
in a sandy ravine.
From there, undercover,
she scopes the marine.

Stingrays are related to sharks and have no bones, only cartilage. They are flat fish with large pectoral fins, making their bodies appear round or diamond-shaped. Some rays have thorny patches on their skin to discourage predators.

A stingray's eyes are on top of its body and its mouth is underneath. Its teeth are fused into bony jaws, which are very strong for crushing food. Stingrays eat worms, mussels, tube anemones, shrimps, crabs, and small fish that they stir up from the ocean floor.

Stingrays are a great example of "countershading" — they are darkly colored on top, so when they are seen from above, they blend in with the ocean depths; and they are lighter on their bellies,

Sting, Ray P.I.

RAY-BAY

so they are camouflaged against the sunlit surface when seen from below. Stingrays often rest nestled into the sandy bottom where they are virtually hidden from view.

The stingray gets its name from the venomous spine on its long tail, which it uses only for protection. Although typically not aggressive, a stingray can deliver a deep and painful slash to something it feels is threatening.

Because stingrays have spiracles behind their eyes, they do not have to keep moving like sharks do to breathe. Spiracles are holes that are used to run water into a stingray's gills and provide oxygen even while they are not swimming. Stingrays can live 30 to 40 years.

FASCINATING FACTS

HERB SEGARS

One puckered gent,
whose name is Moray,
looks out from his
window of rock every day.

His breathing is shallow.
His eyesight is bad.
This eel's got zeal,
but only a tad.
Still, some say he's creepy.
It's break-my-heart sad.

〜 There are more than 600 kinds of eels. Eels may look like snakes, but they are not. They are long-bodied, slow-swimming bony fish that inhabit tropical and warm waters around the world. They live mostly in coral reefs and rocky areas, taking shelter in cracks and crevices.

〜 A few eel species are diurnal (active during the day), but others, like morays, are nocturnal and hunt mainly at night.

〜 Moray eels can grow up to 10 feet long and weigh 75 pounds. Morays do not shock people with electricity. In fact, "electric eels," which have cells on their bodies that send out small shock waves to help them "feel" their surroundings, do not even live in the ocean — they live in the Amazon Basin of South America.

〜 Eels have poor eyesight but possess a good sense of smell.

〜 They are often communal (live in groups) and don't bother anything except their prey, which is mostly little fish, shrimp, and octopus.

〜 An eel's gills are too small to absorb enough oxygen, so they open and close their mouths to pump more water over their gills.

FASCINATING FACTS

HERB SEGARS

If you need a lifeguard
that's able and strong,
you may pray a dolphin
comes zipping along.

She's smart,
and her talent for surfing is great.
Plus, she uses sonar
to echolocate,
a trait that makes
her navigation first-rate.

Dolphins are mammals that breathe through a single blowhole (nostril) on the top of the head. They have no sense of smell (no olfactory lobe in the brain), but they have a strong ability to taste and keen eyesight in and out of water.

Dolphins also have sonar ability called echolocation: They send out sound waves that bounce off objects and come back to give them a 3-D map of their surroundings.

The dolphin's brain is large and complex. They are extremely smart and even have been seen using fish bones as tools to pry other fish out of crevices. Dolphins communicate with clicks and whistles and can give instructions to other dolphins. Each dolphin has a unique whistle that it uses to identify itself.

Dolphins have been known to save drowning humans. Baby dolphins are born tail first and then the mother pushes up and supports a newborn infant at the surface to breathe. Dolphins will also hold sick or injured members of their herd at the surface when necessary.

Dolphins eat mostly small fish and squid. They can dive to more than 1,000 feet, although the pressure at that depth distorts their body. Dolphins sleep only half their brains at a time.

FASCINATING FACTS

HERB SEGARS

The Disney character Nemo is a clownfish. Clownfish are best known for a symbiotic relationship (partnership) with poisonous, meat-eating animals called anemones. Anemones attach themselves to a reef with suction discs at their base and allow their stinging tentacles to sway with the current and capture prey.

Young clownfish perform a behavior called "anemone rubbing." Protected by thick mucus on its skin, the clownfish moves between the anemone's tentacles, allowing it to sting. Over time, the anemone's chemical structure mixes into the fish's mucus. Eventually, the anemone is unable to detect the fish and quits stinging. From then on the fish can hide in the security of the anemone's tentacles.

The clownfish feeds on the remains of the anemone's victims as well as on debris and dead tissue from its host. In return, the clownfish lures prey to the anemone and fights off intruders. Some have been seen bringing food to the anemone.

Clownfish are named for their bright and distinctive orange, black, and white coloring and their visually silly behavior of scooting in and out of their protective homes.

FASCINATING FACTS

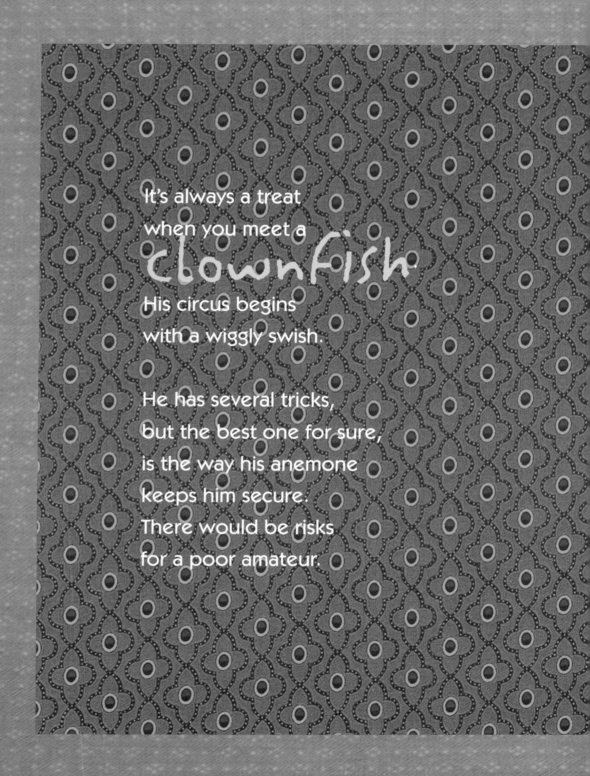

It's always a treat
when you meet a
clownfish
His circus begins
with a wiggly swish.

He has several tricks,
but the best one for sure,
is the way his anemone
keeps him secure.
There would be risks
for a poor amateur.

Sea Lions

can be an unruly crowd,
pushing each other
and barking out loud.

But once in the water,
they're playful indeed.
Agile athletes,
known for their speed,
darting through forests
of rich, green seaweed.

Sea lions are pinnipeds (a term derived from Latin words meaning "fin-footed"). They spend most of their time in the water, but rest and reproduce on land.

Sea lions are intelligent and social mammals. They congregate on land in large groups called colonies, and in the water in smaller groups called rafts. Breeding areas are called rookeries. Wherever sea lions gather, there is usually noisy, persistent barking.

Sea lions are very skilled and fast swimmers, reaching speeds of up to 25 mph in short bursts. Male sea lions can weigh 550 to

750 pounds, and females can weigh up to 250 pounds.

Unlike seals, sea lions have external ear flaps. On land, sea lions use their long, broad front flippers to hold an upright posture.

Because their hip joints allow rotation, they travel with "walking" movements (seals have only ear holes, lie flat on land, and have to lunge forward like caterpillars).

Sea lions are carnivores (meat-eaters) and eat fish, squid, octopus, crabs, clams, and lobsters. They can crush the shells of crustaceans and mollusks with their flat back teeth. They don't chew their food, but swallow it in large chunks or whole.

FASCINATING FACTS

BROOKE BESSESEN

Of the eight pelican species, only the brown pelican is strictly a marine bird, inhabiting coastal areas in North and South America.

A pelican has large, webbed feet and a broad body. Its wingspan can reach more than 7 feet. It also has a long bill with a tremendous lower pouch, which can hold 3 gallons (its stomach can only hold 1 gallon).

Pelicans eat mid-sized fish by making plunging dives from heights of 20 to 60 feet and scooping fish into their pouch. Their chests are full of air sacs that can be inflated before diving and cushion the impact with the water. Once on the surface, they drain the water out of the pouch and swallow the fish before flying off.

Pelicans nest in colonies on small coastal islands. Their nests are flimsy piles of sticks, reeds, bones, and seaweed. Females lay one to three eggs and both parents care for the young.

Brown pelicans reach adult plumage (feather coloring) by about 3 years old and can live more than 25 years.

The brown pelican was once endangered in the United States because of a pesticide called DDT. Their numbers are still extremely low in some areas of the world.

FASCINATING FACTS

BROOKE BESSESEN

From high in the sky,

he begins to pitch down …

Then Pelican dives

like a stuntman of brown.

He plunges straight into

the ocean below.

Thank goodness for airbags,

which soften the blow.

Then he scoops up his catch.

Wow! This guy's a pro.

Down where it's dark
like the pitch black of night,
an angler
fish dangles
her small lure of light.

She knows that her dinner
just cannot resist,
and when it comes closer …
well, you get the gist.
How cool that these
deep water creatures exist.

Usually found in the Atlantic and Southern oceans, deep sea angler fish live in the deepest waters, called the aphotic (or midnight) zone, where it is entirely dark, the water pressure is severe, and the temperature is near freezing. Ninety percent of the ocean is in the midnight zone, although few animals can live there.

Well-suited for the incredible pressure at such extreme depth, deep sea angler fish have soft bones and thin, gelatinous skin. They have gaping mouths with long, sharp teeth.

Deep sea anglers are sexually dimorphic (males and females look different). Only the female has a "fishing pole" — a spine of the dorsal fin that looks like a lure. To make the lure visible in the darkness, the tip has a light-producing organ. Other fish are attracted to the bait, come too close, and get eaten.

The male deep sea angler fish is very small and lives as a parasite on the female's body. He attaches himself by biting the female, and his mouth fuses with her skin. The bloodstreams of the two fish become connected so he is dependent on her for nourishment. His eyes grow smaller until they eventually disappear, along with his internal organs, and his only role becomes to help her reproduce.

FASCINATING FACTS

FASCINATING FACTS

HERB SEGARS

An octopus has the largest and most complex brain of any invertebrate. In aquariums, it has learned to solve mazes, unscrew jar lids to retrieve food, and even mimic an octopus in another tank. Because it has no skeleton, it can squeeze through very narrow spaces.

An octopus is totally deaf but has well-developed eyes that can rotate 180 degrees. It has a mantle (body) and 8 long tentacles (arms), each with two rows of suction cups. In the center underneath, its beaked mouth is shaped like a parrot's. Octopuses have blue blood and a short life span of only 2 to 3 years.

An **OCTOPUS** mind
is as sharp as a tack.
He's ever so clever,
a real brainiac.

And he can change colors
from brown hues to pink,
but if danger's close
and there's no time to think,
he squirts out dark ink,
and is gone in a blink.

An octopus is a mollusk. It eats mainly crustaceans and other mollusks, often luring them by wiggling the tip of a tentacle like a worm. Once it catches its prey, the octopus bites it. Some species have salivary glands that secrete a paralyzing toxin.

When startled or in danger, an octopus can squirt a harmless dark liquid from its ink gland to confuse would-be predators while the octopus makes its escape. It can also change color for camouflage.

The female octopus lays gelatinous strands of eggs that resemble grapes on the vine, and guards them until they hatch. She doesn't eat for the entire time she cares for the young, and some mothers have been known to starve to death.

So, next time you gaze
'cross the **ocean**
so broad,
you'll know the flat surface
is just a façade.

Under, a wonderland,
anciently old,
is brimming with
beautiful life to behold,
places and faces
more precious than gold.